D1267040

SEVEN
SUMMITS

VINSON MASSIF

Amie Jane Leavitt

AV² provides enriched content that supplements and complements this book. Weigl's AV² books strive to create inspired learning and engage young minds in a total learning experience.

Your AV² Media Enhanced books come alive with...

Audio
Listen to sections of the book read aloud.

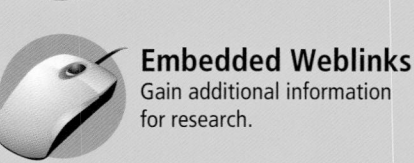

Video
Watch informative video clips.

Embedded Weblinks
Gain additional information for research.

Try This!
Complete activities and hands-on experiments.

Key Words
Study vocabulary, and complete a matching word activity.

Quizzes
Test your knowledge.

Slideshow
View images and captions, and prepare a presentation.

... and much, much more!

Go to www.av2books.com, and enter this book's unique code.

BOOK CODE

AVU23534

AV² by Weigl brings you media enhanced books that support active learning.

Published by AV² by Weigl
350 5ᵗʰ Avenue, 59ᵗʰ Floor
New York, NY 10118
Website: www.av2books.com

Library of Congress Cataloging-in-Publication Data
Names: Leavitt, Amie Jane, author.
Title: Vinson Massif / Amie Jane Leavitt.
Description: New York : AV2 by Weigl, [2019] | Series: Seven summits | Includes index. | Audience: Grade 4 to 6.
Identifiers: LCCN 2019009588 (print) | LCCN 2019017877 (ebook) | ISBN 9781791114206 (multi User ebook) | ISBN 9781791114220 (single User ebook) | ISBN 9781791114190 (hardcover : alk. paper) | ISBN 9781791114213 (softcover : alk. paper)
Subjects: LCSH: Vinson Massif (Antarctica)--Juvenile literature. | Natural history--Antarctica--Juvenile literature. | Mountain ecology--Antarctica--Juvenile literature.
Classification: LCC GB555 (ebook) | LCC GB555 .L43 2019 (print) | DDC 919.89--dc23
LC record available at https://lccn.loc.gov/2019009588

Printed in Guangzhou, China
1 2 3 4 5 6 7 8 9 0   23 22 21 20 19

052019
102318

Editor: Katie Gillespie
Designers: Tammy West and Ana Maria Vidal

SEVEN SUMMITS
VINSON MASSIF

CONTENTS

A Peak of Distinction

Imagine standing on top of the highest point on the very bottom of the world. That is exactly what happens when climbers reach the **apex** of Antarctica's highest peak, Vinson **Massif**. This snow-blanketed mountain rises to an elevation of 16,050 feet (4,892 meters).

Vinson Massif is not a lone mountain soaring into the southern sky. It is part of a family of rugged peaks called the Ellsworth Mountains, which boast six of Antarctica's highest mountains. These also include Mount Tyree at 15,919 feet (4,852 m), Mount Shinn at 15,292 feet (4,661 m), Mount Gardner at 15,003 feet (4,573 m), Mount Craddock at 14,331 feet (4,368 m), and Mount Epperly at 14,301 (4,359 m).

Not much of Mount Tyree has been explored yet. The mountain was first discovered in January 1958.

Mount Shinn was named in honor of Conrad Shinn, a U.S. Navy pilot who landed the first plane at the South Pole, on October 31, 1956.

MAP OF VINSON MASSIF

Atlantic
Ocean

ANTARCTICA

★ **Vinson Massif**

• South Pole

LEGEND
☐ Water
☐ Antarctica
☐ Ice Shelves
★ Vinson Massif

N
W E
S

400 MI

MAP
SCALE 0 ⊢———————⊣
400 KM

Pacific
Ocean

VINSON MASSIF FACTS

• Vinson Massif was named after Carl Vinson, an American congressman who supported research in Antarctica.

• *Massif* is a French word that is pronounced "mass-eef." It means "massive" in English.

• Vinson Massif is also known as Mount Vinson.

• The first successful ascent of Vinson Massif was led by Nicholas Clinch. His team reached the summit on December 17, 1966.

Where in the World?

Antarctica is Earth's southernmost continent. Its closest landmass is the southern tip of South America. As a continent, Antarctica sets many records, for being the windiest, coldest, driest, and most desolate. It is also the highest of all the continents. The average elevation on Antarctica is 8,202 feet (2,500 m). Antarctica is the fifth-largest continent. It is larger than both Europe and Australia.

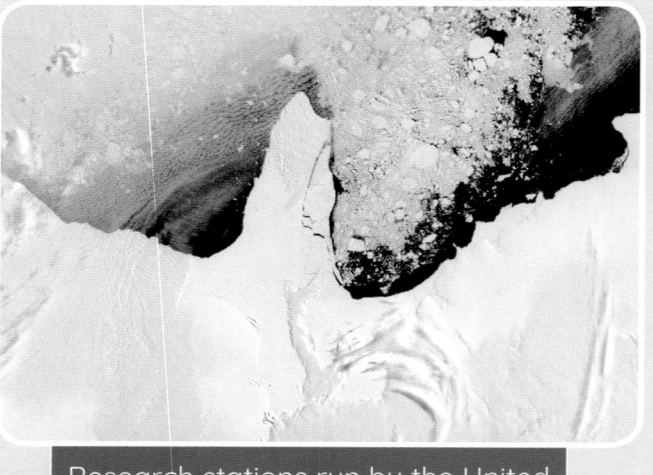

Research stations run by the United States, Argentina, and the United Kingdom have all been operated on the Filchner-Ronne Ice Shelf.

Vinson Massif is located in western Antarctica, about 750 miles (1,200 kilometers) from the South Pole. It is just south of two famous landmarks. These are the Filchner-Ronne Ice Shelf and the Antarctic **Peninsula**.

Covered in ice, the 800-mile (1,300-km) long Antarctic Peninsula extends north from Antarctica toward South America.

Puzzler

Vinson Massif is the highest mountain on the continent of Antarctica. The highest mountains for all of the continents, sometimes called the "seven summits," are listed below. Using an atlas or the internet, match the mountain to the correct continent.

CONTINENTS
1. North America
2. South America
3. Europe
4. Antarctica
5. Asia
6. Australasia
7. Africa

MOUNTAINS
A. Carstensz Pyramid
B. Mount Aconcagua
C. Mount Kilimanjaro
D. Mount Everest
E. Mount Elbrus
F. Denali
G. Vinson Massif

HINT: Visitors often come here to see wildlife such as wolves, grizzly bears, Dall sheep, moose, and caribou.

HINT: The Sherpa people call this mountain *Chomolungma*, which means, "Goddess Mother of the World."

HINT: Many different types of birds live near this mountain, including the condor and purple eagle.

HINT: This peak is a dormant volcano with twin cones. It is also the highest peak in the Caucasus mountains.

HINT: This mountain was named for a Dutch seaman who was the first European to see it.

HINT: This peak is 13 miles (21 km) long, 8 miles (13 km) wide, and about 3 miles (5 km) high.

HINT: This mountain has a wide variety of plant life, including tropical rainforest, shrubland, desert, and an arctic summit.

A: 1.F 2.B 3.E 4.G 5.D 6.A 7.C

A Trip Back in Time

Vinson Massif is extremely old. It started forming millions of years ago, when layers of rock were deposited on top of each other. The mountain's oldest rocks date back more than 500 million years. Over time, the rocks on Vinson Massif have been eroded and sculpted by **glaciers**, giving them their jagged appearance.

Fossils have been discovered in the Ellsworth Mountains near Vinson Massif. These fossils include **species** of trilobites, mollusks, and even a feathery, fern-like plant. These are not the types of fossils one would expect to find in the layers of high mountains on a frigid, icy continent. This shows that Antarctica was once located in a much warmer part of the world. It also supports the scientific theory of **plate tectonics**.

Vinson Massif is made up mostly of metamorphic rocks. This type of rock is formed when layers of sediment are heated and compacted.

How the Ellsworth Mountains Formed

The Ellsworth Mountains are 217 miles (350 km) long and 50 miles (80 km) wide. They are part of a huge rock chunk, sometimes referred to as a crustal block. Crustal blocks form when a section of Earth's **crust** breaks off at a fault, or crack, in Earth's surface. Pressure from within Earth causes some crustal blocks to get pushed or tilted vertically, forming mountains. These mountains, such as the Ellsworth Mountains, have a steep front side and a sloping back side.

There are at least four crustal blocks in western Antarctica. In between these crustal blocks are large ice sheets. Scientists believe that some of this ice could extend well below the ocean's surface. If this is the case, these crustal blocks are actually an **archipelago** in a sea of ice.

Within the Ellsworth Mountains is the Sentinel Range. Vinson Massif is found on the southern part of its main ridge.

Cold Weather Plants

The surface of Vinson Massif is permanently covered in ice and snow, and the weather conditions are extremely cold and dry, making it difficult for plant life to exist. Most of Antarctica can be described this way, too. In fact, less than 1 percent of Antarctica's land is capable of supporting plant life. On these small pockets of land, certain types of simple plants thrive. Many species of lichens, mosses, liverworts, fungi, algae, seaweed, and phytoplankton grow in Antarctica and its surrounding seas.

These living things can develop **adaptations**, which allow them to survive the extreme conditions. For example, snow algae grow underneath sea ice or on top of glaciers. These colonies of single-celled organisms can transform a snowbank from brilliant white into a carpet of pinks, reds, oranges, grays, blues, and greens. Some snow algae smell like watermelon. Antarctica's harsh climate also makes it difficult for plants to grow quickly. Lichens, for instance, can take between 100 and 1,000 years to grow even 0.4 inches (1 centimeter).

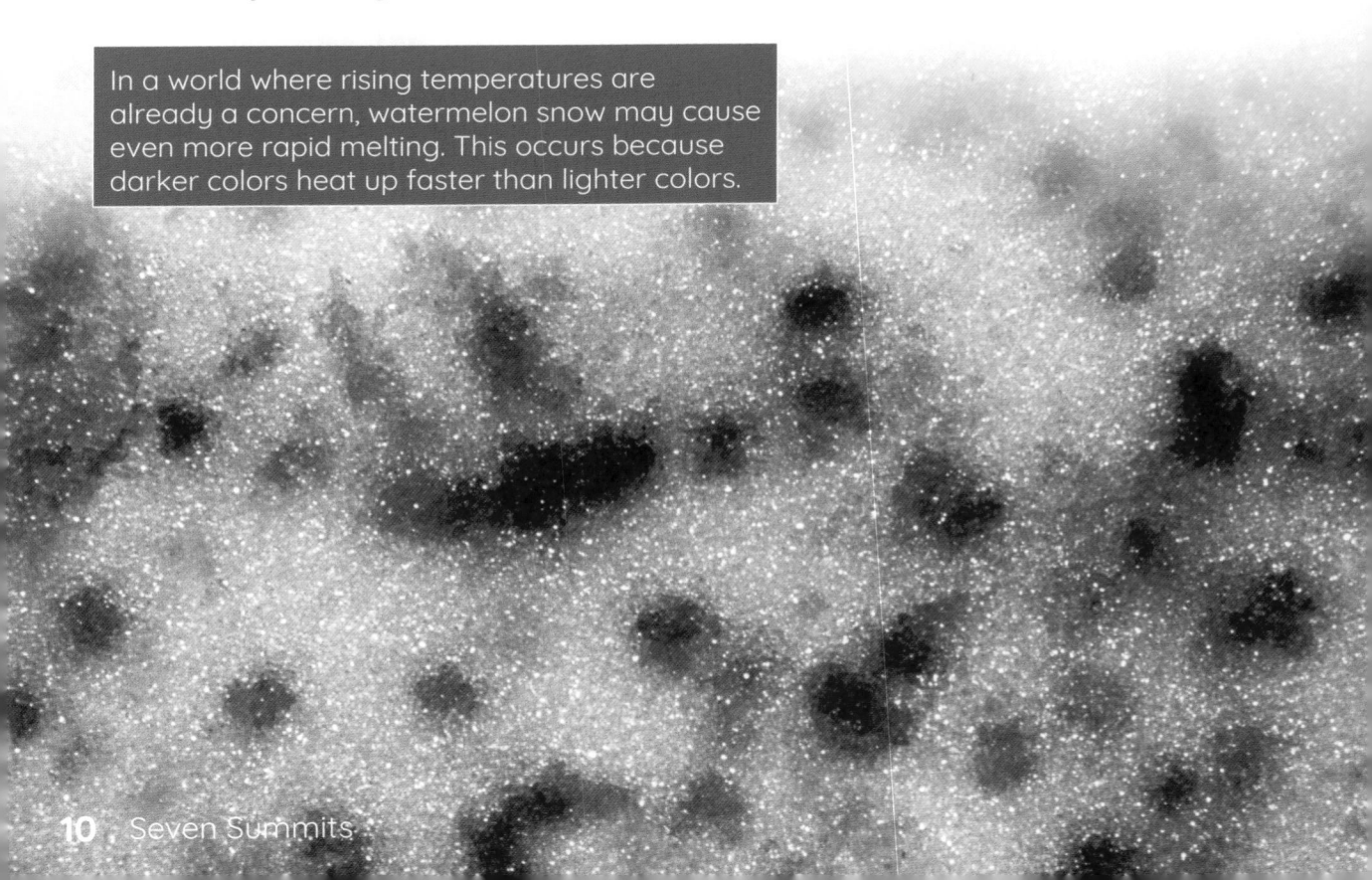

In a world where rising temperatures are already a concern, watermelon snow may cause even more rapid melting. This occurs because darker colors heat up faster than lighter colors.

Flowering Plants

Approximately 900 different types of flowering plants grow in the Arctic. However, only two flowering plants grow in the Antarctic. These are Antarctic Hair Grass and Antarctic Pearlwort.

Antarctic Hair Grass is emerald green and has fine, blade-shaped leaves. It grows in short clumps, in between rock crevices. This plant's tiny flowers remain closed and form seeds in the summer. Antarctic Hair Grass has deep roots, which help it stay anchored in place.

Antarctic Pearlwort grows in between rocks as well. While Antarctic Hair Grass is completely green, Antarctic Pearlwort is covered in tiny yellow bell flowers. This plant is thick, dense, and spongy like a pillow.

Both Antarctic Hair Grass and Antarctic Pearlwort grow on the Antarctic Peninsula.

Snow-loving Animals

Just as it is difficult for plants to grow on Vinson Massif, the amount of animals in this region is also limited. However, some parts of Antarctica are home to specific animal species. The Antarctic Peninsula, for example, is a breeding ground for seals, sea lions, seabirds, penguins, and a variety of insects.

In addition, many animals live in the waters surrounding Antarctica. These include whales, krill, and squid. On the ocean floor around Antarctica, there are even giant sea spiders that measure as large as a dinner plate.

Springtime brings the seabirds. Roughly 100 million birds **migrate** to the Antarctic coastline for breeding reasons. The Arctic tern is one of these. This 4-ounce (113-gram) bird has the longest migration of any bird in the world. It has been reported to travel a round-trip distance of more than 50,000 miles (80,000 km).

The Arctic tern eats fish, insects, and crustaceans such as crab and lobster.

Famous Residents

Penguins only live in the southern hemisphere. It is estimated that 12 million penguins live on the continent of Antarctica. All penguins share certain characteristics. For instance, they have wings that are used to swim instead of fly. When they glide through the water, penguins resemble underwater speedboats. Penguins are carnivores, with a main diet of krill, fish, and squid.

The Emperor Penguin is the largest of all the penguins. Although individual birds vary in size, Emperor Penguins can sometimes be as tall as 4.2 feet (1.3 m) and weigh up to 99 pounds (45 kilograms). Once an Emperor Penguin egg is laid, the female places it on the male's feet. Then, he keeps it warm and safe while she goes out to hunt for the family's food.

Penguins are hatched from eggs. They live together in colonies of thousands of birds.

Early Explorers

For thousands of years, people suspected that there was a continent at the bottom of Earth. However, it is believed that no one saw Antarctica until 1820. That year, Russian, British, and American explorers all saw different parts of the continent.

For the next century, people explored various parts of Antarctica. The British set up the first base on the continent in 1898 and recorded many scientific observations. In 1911, Norwegian explorer Roald Amundsen and British explorer Robert F. Scott raced to be the first to reach the South Pole.

An American explorer named Lincoln Ellsworth became the first to fly across Antarctica in 1935. He was also the first known person to see the Ellsworth Mountains, which is why they were named after him. No one saw them again until January 1958, when they were rediscovered during an aerial survey. Between 1958 and 1961, the U.S. Navy and the United States Geological Survey (USGS) organized both ground and aerial surveys of the mountains, and Vinson Massif was mapped and measured.

Amundsen's team was the first to reach the South Pole. They arrived on December 14, 1911.

Biography
Lincoln Ellsworth (1880–1951)

William Linn Ellsworth was born on May 12, 1880, in Chicago, Illinois. From a young age, he had a great interest in the outdoors. In 1905, after spending a few years working in Canada, Ellsworth was hired at a gold mine in Alaska. It was here that he first caught a glimpse of the unknown Arctic. In the years that followed, news of expeditions to the North and South Poles sparked his interest. It would not be long until Ellsworth would undertake his own polar journeys.

In 1925, Ellsworth embarked upon a polar air expedition with Amundsen. They had to make an emergency landing and were thought to be lost, but after 30 days, they were able to fly back to Norway with all six members of their party. In 1926, along with Italian explorer Umberto Nobile, Ellsworth and Amundsen made another journey, in an airship called the *Norge*. This time, they set a record for the first traverse of the Arctic basin. After his record-setting trip across Antarctica in 1935, Ellsworth flew over the continent again, in 1939.

Ellsworth was originally named after his uncle, William Linn. He changed his name to Lincoln at an early age.

Massifs Around the World

As their name suggests, massifs are extremely large. They can be found on Earth's surface and under water. In addition to Vinson Massif, there are many other examples of massifs around the world.

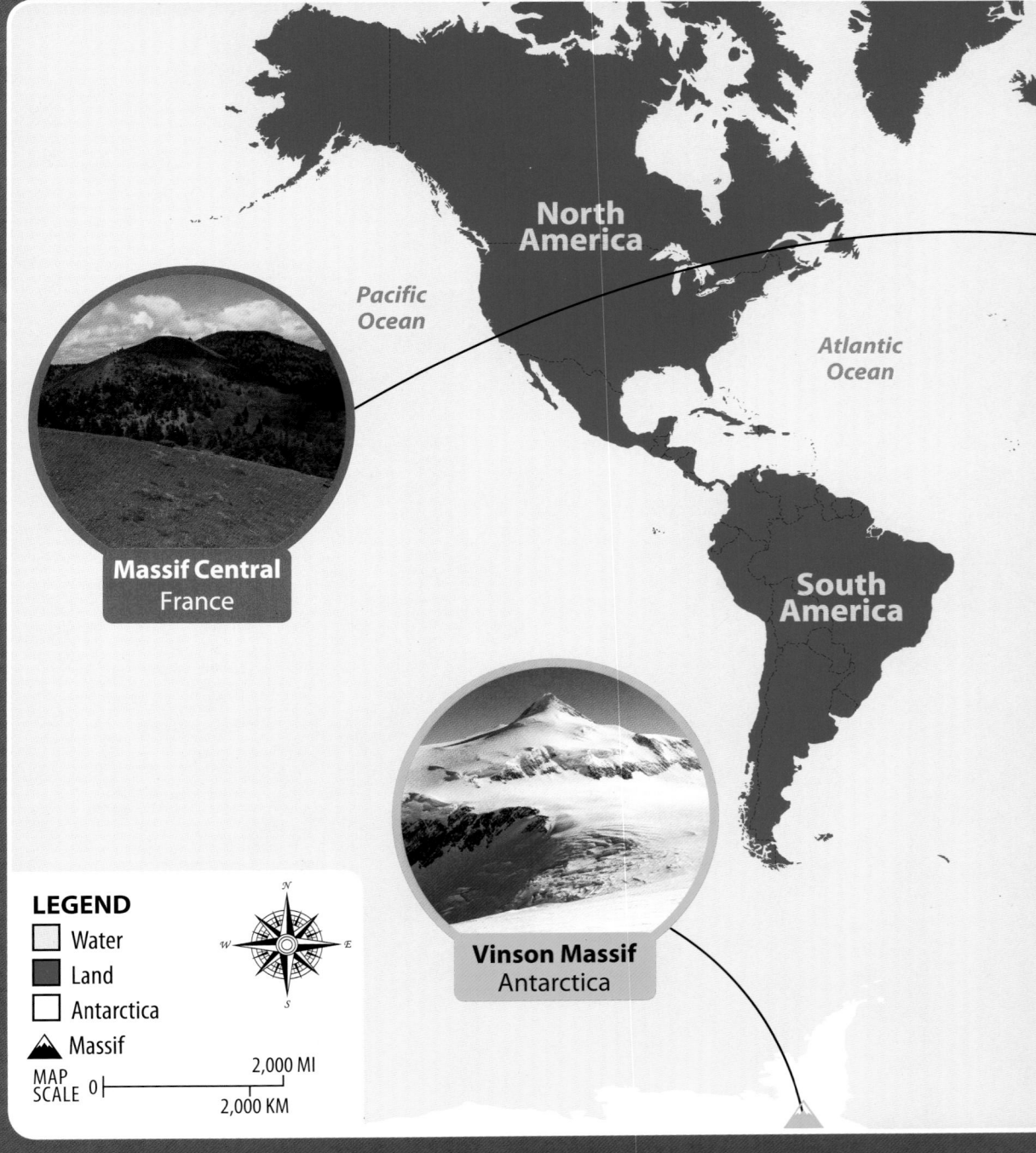

North America

Pacific Ocean

Atlantic Ocean

Massif Central
France

South America

Vinson Massif
Antarctica

LEGEND

☐ Water
☐ Land
☐ Antarctica
▲ Massif

MAP SCALE   0 ⊢————————— 2,000 MI
                    2,000 KM

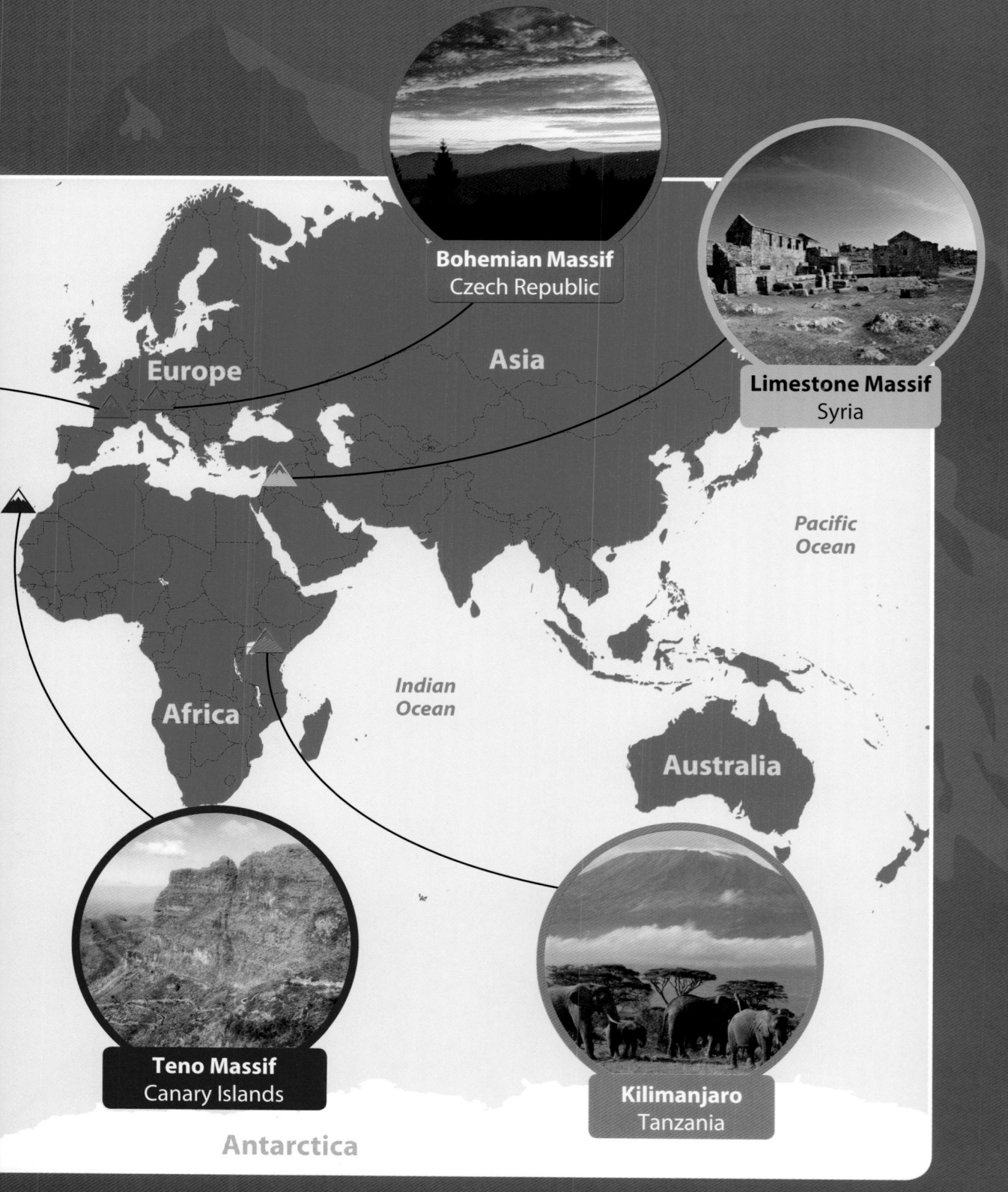

Bohemian Massif
Czech Republic

Limestone Massif
Syria

Europe

Asia

Pacific
Ocean

Indian
Ocean

Africa

Australia

Teno Massif
Canary Islands

Kilimanjaro
Tanzania

Antarctica

Studying the Southern Continent

Since the discovery of Antarctica, people around the world have been fascinated by the science of the snowy "White Continent." Scientists come from all over the globe to study in Antarctica's unique environment. Geologists examine rocks to learn more about Earth's history. Astronomers flock to Antarctica to gaze into the heavens.

Since Antarctica has no sunlight for six months of the year, and it does not have any light **pollution**, the continent has ideal conditions for such research. Climate scientists come to study the oceans and ice sheets, to see how humans are impacting the planet. Biologists come to study the wildlife and learn more about how these animals survive in extreme places.

In 1959, it was agreed by 12 nations that Antarctica would only be used for peaceful purposes, including exploration, research, and scientific discovery. There are currently about 40 year-round stations in Antarctica. Generally, scientists only stay for a few months on the continent, but some stay as long as one to two years.

The flags of the original Antarctic Treaty nations fly at McMurdo Station.

McMurdo Station

The largest research community in Antarctica is the United States' McMurdo Station. It can support up to 1,258 residents at any given time. McMurdo is located on the rocky coastline of Ross Island. It has a harbor where cargo ships can dock and an airfield where ski-equipped cargo planes can land on ice strips. Supplies in Antarctica have to be brought in. They are typically delivered during the summer months.

In February 2019, a major renovation of McMurdo Station was approved. Called Antarctica Infrastructure Modernization for Science (AIMS), the 10-year project will improve energy efficiency and increase safety. Although there are currently more than 100 buildings at McMurdo Station, the new project will consolidate them into only six main structures.

The AIMS project will be the first significant update to McMurdo Station in more than 60 years.

Vinson Massif Timeline

Prehistoric

500 million years ago The **Transantarctic Mountains** form.

500 MILLION YEARS AGO

190 million years ago The Ellsworth Mountains form.

650 AD Maori legend tells of a war canoe that sailed to the frozen southern ocean.

650 AD

Exploration

1820 Explorers from Russia, Great Britain, and the United States, each see different parts of Antarctica for the first time.

1898 The British set up the first base in Antarctica and record scientific observations.

1911 Roald Amundsen and Robert F. Scott race to be the first to reach the South Pole.

1935 Lincoln Ellsworth is the first to fly across Antarctica.

1911

1935

Development

1943–1945 During World War II, the British set up bases and begin conducting scientific studies.

1946 The United States launches Operation Highjump, the largest Antarctic expedition in history.

1946

1949–1952 A team of European scientists work together to study Antarctic climate conditions.

1958–1961 The U.S. Navy and USGS organize ground and aerial surveys of the Ellsworth Mountains. Vinson Massif is mapped and measured.

1959 The Antarctic Treaty is signed by 12 nations. It says that the continent should only be used for peaceful purposes, such as science and research. Today, the treaty has 53 parties.

1959

1966 Nicholas Clinch leads the first successful ascent of Vinson Massif.

1985 Scientists notice a steep decline in ozone levels over Antarctica.

1991 The Environmental Protocol is signed, which protects the environment of Antarctica.

Present

2001 The first successful climb to the summit of Vinson Massif via the eastern route takes place.

2012 Jordan Romero, age 15, becomes the youngest person to climb Vinson Massif.

2012

2001

2018 Scientists use radar to discover mountain ranges and vast canyons buried beneath the Antarctic ice.

Key Issue: Protecting Vinson Massif

Up to 5,000 scientists come to Antarctica each year, and since 2017, tourists have numbered around 50,000 per year. All of these people pose an increased risk of damage to Antarctica's pristine wilderness. With one footstep, a person might accidentally destroy hundreds of years of fragile plant growth.

People might also bring non-native species with them to Antarctica, even unintentionally. These foreign species could start to grow, choking out delicate native plants. Non-native animals could be a problem, too. If rodents or insects are transported to Antarctica via shipping vessels and airplanes, they might wreak havoc on this special environment.

Where there are people, there is also waste. Bathroom waste can cause disease if not disposed of properly. In addition, people use many products while in Antarctica. Whatever waste is left from these products could form huge landfills in Antarctica.

Some tourists embark in small boats, which dock on shore. There, they can walk among the penguins, and get a closer look at the seals.

Many of the world's nations have agreed on rules to protect Antarctica. No one is allowed to dump pollution into the sea. People must protect the wildlife and not bring non-native species onto the continent. All waste must be treated or hauled away. Protecting Antarctica is a continual process, and careful attention is necessary to keep it unspoiled for future generations.

Tiny bristles, seeds, and thorns from other places can get stuck on a person's clothing or shoes.

SHOULD PEOPLE BE ALLOWED TO VISIT ANTARCTICA?

YES	NO
It is an important place for scientific research.	Antarctica gets damaged when people walk on it.
If they follow the rules, tourists should be allowed to see this place and the amazing animals that live here.	When people bring non-native plants and animals with them, Antarctica's wildlife may be harmed.
When people see new places, they often want to help protect them.	People can easily learn about Antarctica by reading books or watching videos.

Taking an Antarctic Vacation

More and more people are skipping their tropical vacations, and are going to frozen Antarctica instead. Those who visit the seventh continent are encouraged to travel with a company that is a member of the International Association of Antarctica Tour Operators. This organization helps keep visitors safe on their journey, while protecting the environment at the same time.

Most of the tourists who visit Antarctica are from the United States. The next largest groups are from China and Australia. Many tourists sail around the continent on large cruise ships, in order to see the ice formations and rugged coastline. Some people even opt to visit the field stations or fly further inland to see the South Pole.

People can only visit Antarctica in the summer months. Winter is not only dark, but extremely cold, and the ocean around Antarctica freezes over. Most tourists coming by boat start their journey from the town of Ushuaia, Argentina. Those who fly in often travel from Cape Town, South Africa.

Tourists to Antarctica must take care. Loud sounds and flashing cameras may disturb animal colonies and migrating birds.

Skiing Antarctica

Some people like an unusual adventure when they travel to Antarctica. Once they reach land, they may strap on cross country skis and trek across the landscape. Tourists can visit the field stations, then journey on to the South Pole.

This voyage can be quite treacherous. Winds blow violently and the temperatures are often cold. Many skiers journey about 600 miles (965 km). They must pull their own sled with supplies behind them the entire way.

Other thrill seekers opt for downhill adventures. They climb steep slopes and then ski or snowboard down them. This type of trip is certainly not for everyone, but it can be very rewarding and exciting.

Downhill adventurers should be physically fit and have experience skiing down steep, black-diamond slopes.

Modern-day Mountaineering

People come to Vinson Massif from all over the world to have the adventure of their lives. Many climbing teams meet in Punta Arenas, Chile. From there, they typically fly 4.5 hours to Antarctica's Union Glacier Camp. Then, they fly to Vinson Base Camp, which features small tents for sleeping and a dining tent.

Next, the climbers begin their way up Vinson Massif. They spend a few days acclimatizing along the way. This means that they must get used to the air at higher altitudes, otherwise they might get very sick. It takes about eight days to make the round-trip climb from base camp to the summit.

Along the way, climbers can experience extremely cold temperatures, as low as -40° Fahrenheit (-40° Celsius). In strong windstorms, the temperatures can feel even colder. Climbers are on the move for about eight hours a day, pulling a sled loaded with supplies.

Even though Vinson Massif is a challenging climb, for many, the view from the top of the bottom of the world is all worth it.

Preparing for the Climb

People have to be physically fit in order to climb one of the Seven Summits. One way to prepare is to run up and down plenty of stairs. People may also go for long runs, dragging a heavy sled or huge truck tire behind them. This helps build their muscles, and strengthens their heart and lungs.

Climbers also need certain equipment with them on the climb. They must have ropes, ice axes, several layers of clothing, face coverings, cleated boots, and goggles. They also have to carry all of the food they need for the trip, a small tent, and sleeping gear.

It takes strength, endurance, and a tolerance of high altitudes to climb the Seven Summits. People who attempt such a feat must work hard to condition their bodies.

What Have You Learned?

True or False?

Decide whether the following statements are true or false. If the statement is false, make it true.

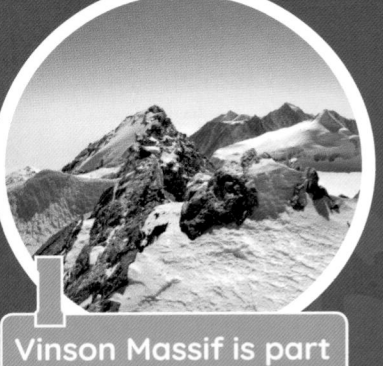

1 Vinson Massif is part of the Ellsworth Mountain range.

2 Australia is the closest landmass to Antarctica.

3 The Arctic tern lives in Antarctica all year long.

4 Antarctica was once in a warmer part of the world.

5 Many climbing teams meet in the country of Brazil.

6 Some scientists study the stars from Antarctica.

ANSWERS

1. True. Vinson Massif is the highest peak in the Ellsworth Mountains. **2.** False. South America is the closest landmass to Antarctica. **3.** False. The Arctic tern migrates to Antarctica for breeding reasons. **4.** True. This was determined by the discovery of fossils. **5.** False. Climbing teams usually meet in the country of Chile. **6.** True. The continent has ideal conditions for such research.

Short Answer

Answer the following questions using information from the book.

1. What are two ways that people can harm Antarctica?
2. What are the two types of flowering plants that grow in Antarctica?
3. What do climate scientists study in Antarctica?
4. What are the jobs of female and male Emperor Penguins?
5. When did people see Antarctica for the first time?

Multiple Choice

Choose the best answer for the following questions.

1. What is a fault?
   a. A crack in Earth's surface
   b. A high mountain range
   c. A special type of plant

2. About how many tourists visit Antarctica each year?
   a. 45,000
   b. 50,000
   c. 55,000

3. Where do most tourists who visit Antarctica come from?
   a. China
   b. Australia
   c. The United States

4. Where is Vinson Massif located?
   a. In western Antarctica
   b. Near McMurdo Station
   c. Next to the South Pole

Activity

Modeling a Crustal Block Mountain

Scientists make models all the time. They use them to understand natural events, processes, ideas, and objects. In this activity, you will make a model that will show how a crustal block mountain is formed.

Materials

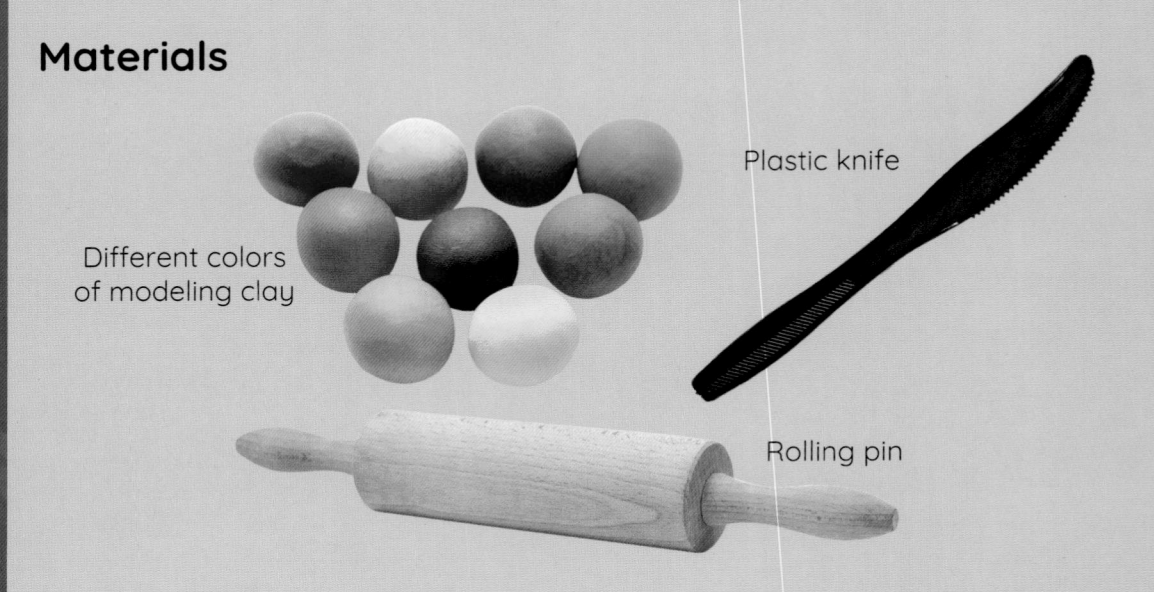

Different colors of modeling clay

Plastic knife

Rolling pin

Instructions

1. Roll out thin layers of each color of clay.

2. Place layers of clay on top of one another until a rectangular block is formed. This represents a section of Earth's crust, with its various layers of rock.

3. Set the block on a flat surface. Using the plastic knife, make a vertical slice through the block. This represents a fault in Earth's crust.

4. You now have two rectangular blocks. Push the end of one block upwards until it is tilted on an angle.

5. Notice how the block is steep on one side and sloped on the other. This shows how a crustal block mountain is formed.

Key Words

adaptations: changes by which an organism or species becomes better suited to its environment

apex: highest point of something

archipelago: a group of islands

crust: top layer of Earth where landmasses and oceans are located

fossils: the impressions of prehistoric plants or animals embedded in rock and preserved in petrified form

glaciers: enormous, slow-moving chunks of ice

massif: a compact portion of a mountain range that contains at least one summit

migrate: to move from one place to another

peninsula: land surrounded on three sides by water

plate tectonics: the theory that Earth's crust is divided into several plates, which move over the mantle

pollution: harmful things that have been added to the environment, in air, land, or water

species: a group of closely related living organisms

Transantarctic Mountains: a system of mountains that divides Antarctica into its western and eastern regions

Index

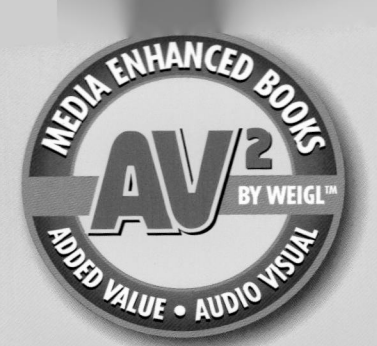

Log on to www.av2books.com

AV² by Weigl brings you media enhanced books that support active learning. Go to www.av2books.com, and enter the special code found on page 2 of this book. You will gain access to enriched and enhanced content that supplements and complements this book. Content includes video, audio, weblinks, quizzes, a slideshow, and activities.

AV² Online Navigation

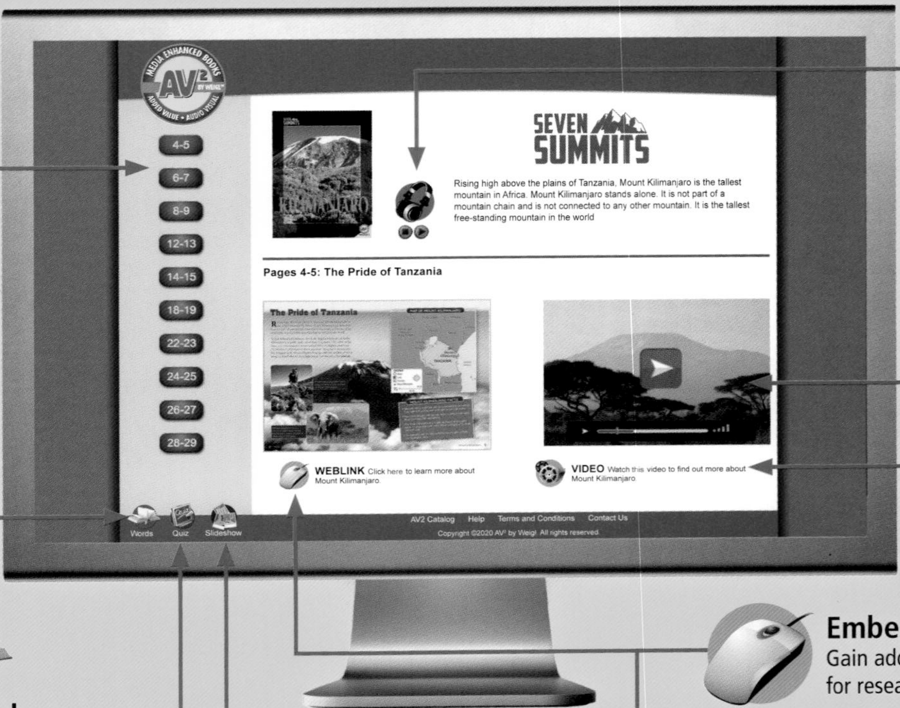

Audio
Listen to sections of the book read aloud.

Book Pages
AV² pages directly correspond to pages in the book.

Video
Watch informative video clips.

Embedded Weblinks
Gain additional information for research.

Key Words
Study vocabulary, and complete a matching word activity.

Try This!
Complete activities and hands-on experiments.

Quizzes
Test your knowledge.

Slideshow
View images and captions, and prepare a presentation.

AV² was built to bridge the gap between print and digital. We encourage you to tell us what you like and what you want to see in the future.

Sign up to be an AV² Ambassador at www.av2books.com/ambassador.